STEVEN CLARK

Mind Control

Your Easy Guide To Understand The World Of Mind Control, Through All Techniques About Mind Control And Body Language

Copyright © 2021 Steven Clark

All rights reserved.

© **Copyright 2021 - All rights reserved.**

The content contained within this book may not be reproduced, duplicated or transmitted without direct written permission from the author or the publisher.

Under no circumstances will any blame or legal responsibility be held against the publisher, or author, for any damages, reparation, or monetary loss due to the information contained within this book. Either directly or indirectly.

Legal Notice:

This book is copyright protected. This book is only for personal use. You cannot amend, distribute, sell, use, quote or paraphrase any part, or the content within this book, without the consent of the author or publisher.

Disclaimer Notice:

Please note the information contained within this document is for educational and entertainment purposes only. All effort has been executed to present accurate, up to date, and reliable, complete information. No warranties of any kind are declared or implied. Readers acknowledge that the author is not engaging in the rendering of legal, financial, medical or professional advice. The content within this book has been derived from various sources. Please consult a licensed professional before attempting any techniques outlined in this book.

By reading this document, the reader agrees that under no circumstances is the author responsible for any losses, direct or indirect, which are incurred as a result of the use of information contained within this document, including, but not limited to, — errors, omissions, or inaccuracies.

Table of Content

Introduction 4

Chapter 1. How Body Language Improves Your Mindset 11

Chapter 2. Proxemics 19

Chapter 3. Muscular Core, Posture, and Breathing 22

Chapter 4. Hand Gestures and Arm Signals 27

Chapter 5. Different Types of People and How They Fit In the Social Circle 33

Chapter 6: Body Language.. 40

Chapter 7. Advanced Techniques to Manipulate Human Psychology 42

Chapter 8. Mind Control 48

Chapter 9. Mind Control Techniques 54

Chapter 10. Influence People With Mind Control 60

Conclusion 66

Introduction

Psychology of Lying

Almost everybody tells a lie once a day or gets lied to. Lying is a part of being a human being with the motive to protect himself against certain situations or to praise oneself. The reasons for lying are endless. Can you remember the very first time you realized that you were lying, or you were lied to?

There is a series of ideas as to why people lie, ranging from saving the hurting of oneself or something else, or with the motive to achieve personal gains. However, science has a different perspective on why people tell lies and the different types of lies. Nobody likes to be lied to, and it's not surprising to find that most liars do not like to be considered as liars.

You wouldn't have any trouble in believing anybody in a perfect world, but unfortunately, it's not perfect, so you need to be cautious about whom to believe and who not to. There are professionals primarily in law enforcement that are trained to detect liars. You don't have to have access to the polygraph machines so that you can understand who is lying to you and who is not. There are many behavioral clues that you could use to know who is telling the truth and who is not.

Detecting deceit will give you the rare opportunity to choose your associates wisely without having to say a word. The body goes into an immense ball of anxiety when a person lies. The trained eye will be able to detect these small variances that occur. Although words may speak their version of the truth, the body never lies. Deceit is the act of covering up the way you truly feel through seeking control. Often, that control is executed in a sloppy manner, thus leading to dominant cues that signal deceit. Whether it's a large lie or a little white lie, the results of dishonesty come with a variety of consequences.

Essentially, people lie as a subconscious form of protection. They are either hiding their negative behavior or protecting their reputations. Even when used to exaggerate a story, they may be attempting to protect the fact that their life is truly boring. They want others to find them enjoyable. Thus, various lies are told.

In general, lying requires more cognitive effort rather than telling the truth because you must work harder and strain to make your information or statement sound authentic. After you have settled on the path of lying, you must remember all the facts, but how? You already changed all facts. Having presented you with the small background about detecting lies, the following are now the various ways you could identify a person lying to you.

Some Liars Are Always Tense and Nervous

It takes a great deal for a liar to pull together fake points to convince you. However, this is not the case with professional liars. These know how to do it just right. But for those who are not used to telling lies, you will quickly notice that their body language is betraying them. On the other hand, a person who tells the truth looks relaxed and happy as far as the story that she is telling is not a sad or painful one.

Some Talk Unusually Slow

If you have ever observed or listened to somebody telling a true story, you might have realized that his or her speech is normal. However, some liars would tend to take quite long before they can respond so that they have a chance to edit their story. They act as if they are trying to be consistent and avoid negative comments. But for other people, it might be hard to detect when they are telling lies, especially salespersons; this is because they have recited lines they keep on mentioning every day with their numerous encounters with customers. You need to keep check of these factors when you are speaking to a person so that you can analyze them and determine when they are telling a lie.

The Hands of a Liar

When people are gesturing and using their hands while telling their stories, this is often seen as a truth-telling sign. However, if the gesturing comes after telling the story, this is often a sign of lying. The mind is so preoccupied with coming up with a story and realistic details that make sense that the mind is too preoccupied to gesture with their hands at the same time that they are talking. Granted, not all people use their hands when talking, but many people do, and this is a simple tactic that the FBI uses and focuses on determining whether someone is lying.

Breathing

Another good indicator if someone is lying is if their breathing suddenly changes. If you ask someone a question and their breathing changes while answering, this is a good sign that they are lying. When somebody is lying, their heart rate upsurges and they turn out to be nervous. It makes them breathe quicker and harder.

Too Still

Another good sign that someone is lying is if they are too still. It is normal for us to move around a bit while talking. It could be shifting in our seat or from foot to foot. Glancing around, hand movements, etc. However, when someone is noticeably too still, this can be a sign of deception. People are often aware that their body language can give them away if they are lying. They think that being fidgety and moving around will give them away. Instead, they do the opposite. They focus very hard on remaining very still so as not to seem fidgety. However, this has the opposite effect than what they were thinking.

Gut Instinct

Lastly, but most importantly, follow your gut instinct. It is probably one of the best ways to figure out if someone is lying to you. People are often very distracted when trying to determine if someone is lying because they focus too hard on the little signs that are supposed to tell you if someone is lying. Frequently, just listen to that other person and then ask yourself if you believe them. We instinctually know when something is "off" about someone. Sometimes we can't even accurately explain what it is or why we feel that way, but we know when something is not genuine. It could be the pitch of their voice, their facial expressions, etc.

Watch the Eyelids

If someone closes his or her eyelids for a long time, it means the person is trying to avoid eye contact. If the person blinks more than three times, it is a sign of nervousness and apprehension that you will catch him or her. If someone uses the hands to cover their eyes, this is another sign that they want to 'block-out' the truth.

Pointing of Eyes

Our eyes point at things we find attractive or where our body wants to go. If you are talking to someone lying, the person will continuously look at the door or watch, signaling the desire to cut short the conversation because they are fearful you will catch the lie.

Avoiding Eye Contact

Breaking eye contact is the most basic way to identify a lie. Someone who has complete confidence about what he or she is saying will never avoid eye contact. However, if someone is lying, he or she will avoid eye contact.

Facial Expressions

Observing facial expressions can help you detect a lie. The most common facial expressions observed in a liar are, dilated pupils, the appearance of lines on the forehead, narrowing of the eyebrows, and blinking eyes. Sweat on the forehead and an angry expression are common with these facial expressions.

Dilated Pupils

Pupil dilation indicates tension and concentration. When someone gets worried about exposure, the pupils unconsciously dilate as they think of ways to hide the lie. If you are talking to someone but unsure if the person is honest or not, look at the person's pupils for answers.

Several key facial indicators may tip you off to whether a person is lying to you. Though none of these are necessarily conclusive in and of themselves, learning to notice these indicators will be your ally when determining if someone is less than trustworthy.

Lines on Forehead

Someone lying may have lines on the forehead because of the stress the person has to bear as they seek ways to cover the lie.

Apart from the facial expression, we can also observe many other gestures in a liar.

Clearing of Throat

If someone is lying to you, he or she will probably clear his or her throat more than once as a nervous tendency to distract from the stress of telling a lie.

Backward Head Movement

When someone is telling a lie, the head could possibly move backward. This gesture occurs as the lying person tries to avoid the source of anxiety because people tend to distance themselves from things they dislike.

Hard Swallowing

The throat of someone who is lying may become dry, and additionally, they may become self-conscious of their swallowing and breathing so as not to give away their deception. Therefore, it is common for a person to swallow hard to bring moisture back to avoid clearing their throat. It is common for people trying to hide a lie.

Statement Analysis to Determine Lie

Analyzing someone's lie through his or her statement is the last step in lie detection. Sometimes what people say does not support their body language. It allows you to detect lies. People often stammer or talk at a fast pace as a way of trying to avoid discovery.

For instance, if you suspect your classmate stole your money and ask her about it, you notice darting eyes and nervousness in her tone. Her body language does not support her statement that she did not steal the money. It means she is lying and has stolen it or knows who did.

No matter how good a person is at lying, if the person's body language is not supportive of their statement, that person is lying. To identify a liar, analyze someone's body language and determine if it matches the person's statement. If the two contradict, you may have a liar on your hands.

You now have a complete idea of analyzing your target by studying body language, expressions, and gestures. It is just one way, however, to analyze people. If you wish to analyze people more efficiently, then you can use the information you gathered from your body language observations. It will give you a complete understanding of your target's state of mind, personality, habits, tendencies, thought patterns, and general operation mode.

Chapter 1. How Body Language Improves Your Mindset

Our body language is the way we speak with our outside world—and the more significant part of us don't understand, we are doing it! Body language phenomenally affects the center of who you are as an individual. It impacts our posture and physiological well-being, yet it can likewise change our psychological viewpoint, an impression of the world, and others' perception of us.

How Our Body Imparts

We utilize our body language to communicate our musings, thoughts, and feelings; we synchronize body developments to the words we express. We impart purposefully through activities like shrugging our shoulders or applauding just as through inadvertent correspondence like twisting in on ourselves or guiding our feet an alternate way toward the individual we talked about. Before spoken language was made, our body language was the primary technique for correspondence. Our body is our major method to speak with life!

How Can It Influence Our State of Mind?

Our body language is how we interface with our outside world, yet it is likewise how we associate with ourselves. How would you treat yourself? Do you slouch over when you walk, or do you walk tall and satisfied? It is true to say that you are thankful for each development that your body makes for you?

Most likely not; we regularly underestimate our body; we frequently decide to condemn it. Body language can impact our physical body and posture. However, it can likewise change how we are feeling. Having a great attitude can affect misery and cause us to keep up more elevated levels of confidence and energy when confronted with pressure.

An up and coming field of psychology, known as installed comprehension, asserts that the association between our body and our general surroundings doesn't merely impact us. However, we are personally woven into the way that we think.

Four Different Ways You Can Change Your Body Language

The followings are four ways you can change your body language.

Flip Around That Glare!

Grinning and snickering is infectious! A complete report on smiling found that a grin which draws in the mouth and moves the skin around the eyes can enact the cerebrum examples of positive feelings. So, grin and grin frequently! Regardless of whether you are having an awful day, grin at any rate! It may very well assist you with turning the day around!

Collapsing Your Arms

The intersection of the arms is a resistance system to ensure the heart and lungs. We regularly do it when we feel shaky, anxious, or disturbed. The physical obstruction gives others the feeling that we are cut off and detached from them.

The intersection of the arms is a broad idea to be an antagonistic body posture anyway. A few investigations have indicated that crossing the arms can cause individuals to progressively industrious when they feel like stopping.

If you believe you need a little additional lift to take a stab at making some regular mindset boosting homegrown cures like Hyperiforce. It contains concentrates of the bloom hypericum frequently utilized as a treatment for low mind-set and gentle nervousness.

Force Presenting

One of the significant specialists in the zone of body language is Amy Cuddy. She made members remain in high force stances and low force models for two minutes before sending them into a top weight talk with the condition. She estimated levels of the pressure hormone cortisol and the predominance hormone testosterone. The outcomes demonstrated that those remaining in high force present had expanded testosterone degrees and lower cortisol levels than those in little force presents.

Quit Slumping

It may appear glaringly evident; however, slumping not just influences your spine. It can likewise change your state of mind! Indeed, slumping can prompt back agony and an irregular spine arrangement. Intellectually, it can leave you feeling miserable, lacking vitality, and shut off from others. Sitting and standing up straighter can assist with settling back torment just as lift your life and state of mind.

Changing your posture can be trying for your body from the outset, particularly on the off chance you are accustomed to slumping over for significant periods! You may feel muscle hurts in the neck, back, and bears—don't stress, this will pass!

Meanwhile, I'd suggest utilizing Atrogel, a natural relief from discomfort cure containing new concentrates of arnica blossoms.

Improve Your Posture to Improve Your Temperament!

Body language likely isn't the first sport you'd think to look at when experiencing a low state of mind. However, investigating our body language can reveal to us how we are truly feeling. Our body language has an immediate connection to our temperament, similarly that our mindset influences our posture.

Simple ways you can fix your posture to adjust your state of mind:

- Smile when you are having a terrible day!

- Unfold your arms when you feel anxious and permit yourself to be available to circumstances.

- Turning the palms of your hands forward when you walk will urge the shoulders to unwind back as opposed to moving advances.

- Power present before pressure instigating situations like prospective employee meet-ups.

Body Language Signs When Someone Hides Something from You

Untrustworthiness. It happens in many connections—and a great deal of the time, it accomplishes more mischief than anything. It's once in a while ever astute to keep insider facts from your accomplice in a relationship. You never need to keep your accomplice in obscurity about a lot of things in your lives together. That is simply out and out insolent. It shows that you don't regard your accomplice enough to recognize that they are deserving of reality. You are saying that they aren't sufficient to be determined what's genuine—and that is, in every case, terrible in a relationship. You generally need to confess all to your accomplice, particularly about vital issues encompassing your relationship.

Be that as it may, a considerable deal of us are childish. Here and there, reality can be difficult to stomach. Now and then, a fact can place us in an extreme condition of a burden once it's uncovered. So, a great deal of us will turn to lie just to spare our butts. Your man may be blameworthy of doing as such. He may be keeping you out of the loop about something that he ought to be opening up to you.

What's more, that is hazardous for a relationship. You can't hope to make your link work if you're not being taken care of the entirety of the best possible realities. You generally need to ensure that you know all that is going on to don't wind up getting tricked or bushwhacked by anything.

Men aren't generally the best verbal communicators. You may likely know this at this point. Be that as it may, he consistently communicates through his body language and physical developments. His intuitive may be disclosed to you many things about himself without seeing it in any event. You simply need to willingly volunteer to ensure that you spot out the signs when they present themselves. You need to ensure that you keep steady over things in your relationship.

Getting and Understanding Nonverbal Signals

Lauren murmured. She'd quite recently gotten an email from her chief, Gus, saying that the item proposition she'd been taking a shot at would not have been closed down. It didn't bode well. Seven days prior, she'd been in a gathering with Gus, and he'd appeared to be extremely positive about everything. Of course, he hadn't looked, and he continued watching out of the window at something. In any case, she'd recently put that down to him being occupied. Furthermore, he'd said that "the task will most likely stretch the go-beyond."

On the off chance that Lauren had discovered somewhat progressively about body language, she'd have understood that Gus was attempting to reveal to her that he wasn't "sold" on her thought. He simply wasn't utilizing words.

The Most Effective Method to Read Negative Body Language

Monitoring negative body language in others can permit you to get on implicit issues or awful emotions. Along these lines, in this area, we'll feature some negative nonverbal signs that you should pay individual minds to.

Troublesome Conversations and Defensiveness

Troublesome or tense discussions are an awkward unavoidable truth grinding away. Maybe you've needed to manage an annoying client or expected to converse with somebody about their terrible showing. Or then again, perhaps you've arranged a significant agreement.

In a perfect world, these circumstances would be settled tranquility. Be that as it may, regularly, they are entangled by sentiments of apprehension, stress, preventiveness, or even resentment. However, we may also attempt to shroud them; these feelings regularly appear through in our body language. For instance, on the chance that somebody is showing at least one of the accompanying practices, he will probably be withdrawn, uninvolved, or miserable:

- Arms collapsed before the body.

- Insignificant or tense outward appearance.

- The body got some distance from you.

- Eyes depressed, keeping in touch.

- Keeping away from Unengaged Audiences

At the point when you have to convey an introduction or to work together in a gathering, you need the individuals around you to be 100 percent locked in. Here are some "obvious" signs that individuals might be exhausted or unbiased in what you're stating:

- Sitting drooped, with heads sad.

- Looking at something different, or into space.

- Squirming, picking at garments, or tinkering with pens and telephones.

- She was composing or doodling.

Step by Step Instructions to Project Positive Body Language

When you utilize positive body language, it can add solidarity to the verbal messages or thoughts you need to pass; on and help you abstain from imparting blended or befuddling signs. In this segment, we'll portray some fundamental postures that you can embrace to extend fearlessness and receptiveness.

Establishing a Confident First Connection

These tips can assist you in adjusting your body language so you establish an extraordinary first connection:

- Have an open posture. Be loose; however, don't slump! Sit or stand upstanding and place your hands by your sides. Abstain from remaining with your hands on your hips will cause you to seem more significant, conveying animosity or craving to rule.

- Utilize a firm handshake. However, don't become overly energetic! You don't need it to get unbalanced or, more regrettable, excruciating for the other individual. On the chance that it does, you'll likely seem to be impolite or forceful.

- Keep in touch. Try to maintain eye contact with the other person for a couple of moments, one after another. It will give her that you're right and locked in. Be that as it may, abstain from transforming it into a gazing match!

- Abstain from contacting your face. There's a typical discernment that individuals who contact their appearances while addressing questions are being untrustworthy. While this isn't in every case valid, it's ideal to abstain from tinkering with your hair or contacting your mouth or nose, especially if your point is to seem to be reliable.

Chapter 2. Proxemics

Now, imagine that you are standing in front of someone. You can see that they are crossing their arms with hands hidden behind them, their eyes shifting nervously from you to veer off to the left now and then. They shift their weight from foot to foot and struggle to maintain eye contact. Something about the body language of this person makes you uneasy, but you cannot place it. They keep their distance from you, and every time you approach closer, you notice that they are likely to move away.

Body language is good at giving us feelings that tell us to be on edge, offended, or relaxed, but if you do not know what you are reading, you will struggle to understand why you feel that way. It can be difficult to know what someone intends to not put meaning to what they are doing. You can have a general idea of how you want to respond, but it can be incredibly beneficial

Proxemics refers to the distance between yourself and someone else—it is the usage of space between yourself and the world around you. Naturally, people put varying degrees of space between themselves and others. When you are looking to understand proxemics, the best way to do so is to consider it a judgment of the relationship between yourself and those around you. You can also judge others' relationships based upon the distance they put between each other, both vertical and horizontal.

The Use of Vertical Space

Vertical space is what it sounds like—it is the space relative to your position height-wise. When someone utilizes vertical space, they attempt to make themselves taller or shorter, depending on the context. Those who want to make themselves taller may want to be an authority or otherwise as someone that is deserving of respect and compliance. They may even use this space when they are trying to look at others who are taller than them—they simply tilt their heads back to look down their nose at the taller person to create the same impact.

When you make yourself smaller, you typically want to be seen as less dominant for some reason. You may be attempting to shrink down to speak to a child to be understood truly, for example, or you may be lowering yourself to make yourself seem more submissive. In particular, people will pull their chins inward when they want to be smaller because they will then be required to look up through their eyelashes at the other person, even if the other person is taller.

The default, eye level, is deemed to be the most respectful—it marks you and the other person as equals deserving of the same respect and consideration.

The Use of Horizontal Space

In horizontal space, you are looking at how near or far people are to each other. You will use this when you are picking apart the relationships of others. There are four distances used between each other, ranging from intimate distances to public distance.

- The intimate distance: This refers to being as close as possible to the other person. When you are in this position, you are usually touching without trying or close enough to do so. It is typically for young children and parents, or for lovers that are comfortable being this close to each other. Generally speaking, this zone is only about 18 inches away from you.

- The personal distance: Slightly further away than the intimate distance, the personal distance covers about 18 inches away up to about 5 feet around you. It is what people are talking about when they say that you are invading their personal bubbles. This zone is usually reserved for those you like or feel comfortable with, such as friends and family members or children who are too old to be within the intimate zone. The closer you can get to the center, the closer your relationship with that other person.

- The social distance: This is a bit further out. It is the distance you naturally try to maintain with strangers around you or interacting with someone else you do not know. Typically, this is between about 5 and 10 feet. You will use this when you are out and about unless you have no choice otherwise. When you are forced to encroach on this distance, you will most often make it a point to ignore the other person in an attempt to ignore the fact that they are violating those personal boundaries, such as sitting on the bus.

- The public distance is even further out. It refers to anything beyond 12 feet and is reserved for instances in which you speak out toward a crowd. You want to be loud enough that everyone in the crowd can speak, so you want to ensure that people are a bit further away from you so they can see and hear you easier. It is reserved for lectures in classrooms, for example, or in performances.

Chapter 3. Muscular Core, Posture, and Breathing

The best way to find out is to copy your subject's muscular core state. Just look at how their muscles are arranged and try to set yours the same way. There's a good expression, "to carry oneself," and your goal will be to carry yourself just like them. Your copy doesn't have to be identical, just close enough. Hence, you feel close enough to themselves. Imitate them as close to perfection as your present acting skills allow (to be a good judge of character, a good analyst, you don't have to be a good actor, but it helps—remember Sherlock Holmes and his transformations?) It isn't hard—just contract whatever they have acquired and kept it that way!

Now, as we learned to carry ourselves like our subject of study, we must learn to walk like them and breathe like them, or at least pretend to do it, deep inside.

Much can be learned from a human posture and walk: people with bad eyesight recognize and spot their relatives and friends by their silhouette, their stance, their walk in the crowd of hundreds of people, alone, as easy as a person with keen eyesight would. Can you stand or sit as your subject does and feel as comfortable as they seem? Can you breathe like them, at the same rate, with the same depth, following the same intervals?

Try and practice it alone at first, looking at a video of someone else. Soon you'll be able to perform it mentally, running the process almost entirely in your imagination. As soon as your musculature and posture imprint feels identical to that of your subject, as soon as your collective breath sounds like one, it's time to analyze their non-verbal message.

Are they demonstrating the will to move closer, shorten the distance between you—or are they trying to distance themselves from you? Is their posture open towards you (face, chest, and groin unobstructed by limbs) or closed from you? (Folded arms, crossed knees, etc.) If their posture is closed, don't jump to conclusions: they may position themselves this way merely for comfort, not because they'd like to lock themselves away from you. If your object's posture is closed and is comfortable—they are likely an introvert. With extroverts, expect abrupt changes in posture, quick movements ahead (lean towards the person they're speaking to, or reach for them), meant to shorten the distance between them.

Body language is a nation-specific feature of communication—in some countries, it's hardly used, while in the other two conversing's, people may resemble two windmills. Still, you can generally detect the heat of discussion by the amount and smoothness of gesturing, even when watching the speakers from a distance. The rougher, sharper gestures become, the less controlled they are, the higher the conflict's likeliness.

A conflict is something often provoked by the opposition, or a third party, with intent to unsettle us, upset us, or make us lose our temper and act out. Our goal in this situation will be to retain control of ourselves. It doesn't mean suppressing our anger or bottling our frustration. It means dissolving the heat of emotions in the cold presence of our reason. It means starting with controlled breathing, restrained posture, and slow relaxation of the muscle core, resetting it to absolute calm.

A person in control is not someone gritting their teeth, holding reins back—it's the person showing calm restraint and conscious choice of their words and actions. Remember the monkey and the computer? The last one is the analyst; the first one lives for battle and spots a good fight mile away. There's a good use for this quality, too: your instincts will tell you when the situation is about to heat up a bit too much, so your reason could be there in time to prevent unnecessary drama before it has a chance to happen!

The point is neither of the two parts of one's consciousness must be restrained or removed from the interaction. When the reason is cast aside, no civilized communication is possible: any conversation will quickly derail and devolve into something childish, silly, and virtually useless for any purposes but socializing itself. If the moving part is suppressed, the person starts feeling discomfort.

It is a significant point. It happens to be twofold: whenever you spot manifestations of discomfort in yourself or your object, you will know it happens because the primal part, the emotional aspect, is subdued by reason. It may occur when the person's reason doesn't want to give something away, yet their body—heartbeat, breathing, perspiration—seems eager to betray them. Hence, they try and shut it off using reason, forcing themselves under control for some time, after which their animalistic part will inevitably act out. You must have seen how leaving the room after a difficult meeting. Usually, people will be overly childish and agitated. They even exclaiming loudly, pushing each other. At the same time, others are craving some sort of physical gratification. It is all the backlash of self-control imposed by reason. Then it is lifted.

Hence, to stay comfortable, to remain in full control of oneself—which is something you want to practice to become a good restrained analyst—one must never suppress their inner feelings! It's hard to give advice on how your computer could keep your monkey in check, as this is a personal thing, inherent to your character. There's a huge number of venting and confidence-building techniques out there, and you're free to try them all! Just remember this simple rule: by indulging a specific whim of your animal, you grow it, not reduce it. For instance, aggressive behavior does not deplete aggression. On the contrary, it increases your aggressiveness—the same as being afraid will not deplete your fear.

Still, techniques help you drop the level of aggression and overcome fear, from the essential things like counting to ten, naming objects around you mentally, or drinking a glass of water—down to counseling and transcendental meditation. In this book, we'll merely say the solution is out there, and self-control is essential if you want to stay an involved yet unbiased party.

On the other hand, this is what you want to notice in the behavior of your subject: not their controlled, reasonable actions, but their slips, their subliminal telltales, the small movements, expressions, and changes in posture that happen without the subject noticing. How to interpret this body language? The problem is that it's inherent to a particular culture and varies from one individual to another.

Many sources claim they're able to teach you some kind of universal list of telltales. One that enables you to tell the truth from lies, present you with recipes of telling an act from the real deal. But these sources are at best-generalized information. It is sometimes applied to many people. Enough to make it seem true, but not to be applied to just everyone. The truth is, only your own experience, attentiveness, and insight will help you to read another person's body language, for there are as many body languages as there are different people.

For instance, when someone is trying to touch or hide a part of their face—lips, the nose, an ear—it's typically considered a sign of secretiveness, the telltale of a person lying or trying to hide some information from the listener. In many cases, it's indeed so—and still, be careful not to call someone a liar just because they tend to rub their three-day stubble while they're thinking.

Another popular facial feature to be pointed out as a telltale: a genuine smile would cause crinkles around eyes, while a fake smile normally wouldn't. Yet again, in many cases, it may be true—we often hear about "someone smiling while their eyes remain cold." Then again, the experiments show the "smiling eyes" can be faked more or less quickly, and if you were to encounter a sociopathic person, someone good at mimicry—you'd never catch them faking a smile.

Approach tendencies in your subject's posture may mean aggression—or they could mean affection, and only your judgment may discern between the two. If your issue demonstrates avoidance tendencies—this, yet again, could mean an entire spectrum of emotions: apathy, fear, disgust, mistrust, submission, meekness, and so on.

A good analyst would always view the non-verbal signals of their subject as a part of the bigger picture, applying to them the knowledge of this person as a whole. Even a habit as simple as biting one's fingernails—are you sure I bite mine when I'm nervous? It may happen a person tends to stick their thumb in their mouth while they're thoughtful, relaxed, their attention directed inward—miles from feeling nervous!

Always remember: what you see is only half of the picture. Another half, no less important, is what you hear.

Chapter 4. Hand Gestures and Arm Signals

It is important to read gestures in the context of other aspects of body language, but we will explore ways of reading gestures. We all talk with our hands often. For some people, the gesturing matches their message well. Some people do not deploy hand gestures while others overuse hand gestures. Most hand gestures are universal. A person that does not use hand gestures may be seen as indifferent.

For this reason, the audience may feel that one does not care about what the other is talking about. If your hands are hidden, then the audience will find it difficult to trust you. If one's hands are open and the palms wide enough, the individual communicates that they are honest and sincere.

Furthermore, randomly throwing hands in the air while talking may suggest that one is anxious or panicking. Extreme anger will also make one throw their hands in an uncoordinated manner. For further understanding, take time and watch movie characters quarreling, and you will note that most people being accused of something will randomly throw their hands in the air. It is something that they have little control over because most of the body language happens at the subconscious level of the mind. Randomly throwing hands in the air indicates that one is overwhelmed with emotions or has given up defending their position in the argument and has left the argument to the individual who started it.

Additionally, one may point at an object or a person. Pointing as a gesture helps the focus of the speaker and the audience to the focused area. During your school days, you probably saw your teacher's point in a particular direction without speaking until the talking students had to stop. As such, pointing at specific students drew the entire class's attention to their direction, making them become the center of attention, and they had to do a quick self-evaluation and stop talking. All these illustrate that body language communicates tone and emotions just as verbal communication.

Furthermore, pointing while wafting the index finger indicates a warning. When one points the index finger at someone and wafts it up and down, then you are denoting a stern warning and judgment to the individual. It is the equivalent of saying, "this is the last warning." Your parent or teacher may probably have a point and waft gesture to signal a warning that what you are doing is wrong and that you should stop. You might have observed that the police or the lead actor uses the index finger to warn someone in movie characters. The finger signal singles out the individual and reduces the focus to just one aspect of behavior that the speaker wants the target person to understand.

If one spreads all the fingers and holds them together against those of the opposite hand, it indicates strong personal reflection, such as praying or remembering the departed soul. The same gesture can be used when one is focusing the mind during meditation or yoga. The holding of each of your fingers against their peers. On the other hand, it may also indicate feeling humble and thankful for everything. For instance, followers of the Catholic faith frequently use this gesture when praying. The gesture shows humility and thankfulness.

Sometimes one may tap on the head once or continuously. When one taps on the head using a hand or a finger, it indicates the individual is thinking hard or trying hard to recall something. For instance, when speaking and you try to remember what another person said, you might use this gesture. Children often tap their heads once or continuously using one finger or the entire palm to signal attempts to recall something. The gesture is equivalent to saying, "Come on, what it was?" or "Come on, what was the name again!" It is a prop to recall hard.

Similarly, a fully raised palm with fingers spread may indicate that one should stop. When stopping the vehicle on the roadside, one raises one of their palms high up, and it is taken as a sign to stop. The same is true in the sporting environment where raising one palm high up commonly communicates that the playing should stop. When arguing with your partner, if they raise one of their palms, it signifies the other to stop arguing or stop whatever action they are doing.

If one claps, the palms together may indicate applauding the message or the speaker. When the speaker is done speaking, the audience may clap their hands together to mark the message's appreciation or both the message and the speaker. However, when the hands are spontaneously and violently clapped, then it is a message that the audience should stop because what they are doing is unethical or irritating. At home, one of your parents probably clapped their hands suddenly and violently to make you stop as well as draw attention to their presence, especially where you were playing loudly around the house.

Relatedly, if one interlocks one hand against those of the other hands and folding them. The application of this gesture indicates that one is attentive but unease at the same time. During an interview, meeting, or a class session, the audience is likely to interlock their fingers and fold them. In a way, the interlocking of the fingers is supposed to offer assurance to the affected person that he or she is safe. One is likely also to use this gesture when he or she is mentioned negatively. Think of how you reacted when you were mentioned among noisemakers or workers having challenges following the company's rules. Most probably, you interlocked your fingers and folded them.

Additionally, if one feels shy or uncertain, the individual is also likely to interlock their fingers and raise the interlocked fingers when speaking. The gesture in this context appears to give some prop for the affected individual enabling them to navigate the anxiety. The gesture in this context is not just about communicating the affected person's physiological status but as a coping mechanism of sudden anxiety and discomfort of the individual.

Still on body language and focusing on gesture, if one raises both hands behind the head and interlocks the fingers, it acts as a cushion for the head. The gesture indicates that one is feeling casual, tired, or simply not tasked by the current conversation. The gesture may also suggest that the individual is feeling tired by the discussion or the activity. Think of how you react when feeling exhausted when talking to a friend or after watching a movie. You probably raised both of your hands behind the head and interlocked the fingers to act as a headrest. In most cases, when one invokes this gesture, the individual is likely to let the mind allow other thoughts to escape from the current conversation.

Correspondingly, there is the gesture where one lets one of their palms to brush down their faces. The gesture is used to signal deeper thinking, process new contradictory information, or accept humiliation in front of the audience. The gesture suggests surrender. It indicates yielding to inner thoughts or views from the audience that one may have initially opposed. At one point, the class or your friends cornered a speaker facing the speaker to pause and take a minute to admit that he or she may have overlooked some facts about the issue. Probably, the speaker used this gesture to indicate defeat.

On the other hand, to indicate rejection or strong disagreement. It is with both hands with palms broad are waved in an alternating manner to create the letter X. You probably drew the letter X using both hands to indicate that you disagree\what is being proposed in class. For instance, as a kid or as a student, you probably drew letter X to signal rejection that you will not follow instructions when the teacher sarcastically indicated that you should not follow his instructions. The sign also indicates retreat to your inner world to avoid listening or watching what the speaker wants.

For accentuation, when hands are open with palms down, at that point, one is communicating that he or she is certain almost what they are talking about. In case your palms are confronting each other with the fingers together. At that point, you're communicating that you just possess the skill around what you're talking about almost. At that point, there's the approximation gesture performed by holding the hand horizontally with palm down and with fingers forward. After that, tilting the hand to the correct and the cleared out. The guess signal shows that an explanation is to be taken a near appraise of the truth.

Equally important, the gesture with a gentle rocking from left to right means that it is not so good or not so bad. The same gesture indicates that an event is equally likely to end in one of the two ways suggesting that it can go either way. The gesture can signal the other person when a match is going, and the friends are watching in the house, and they do not want to wake up the child through loud talking.

Similarly, the beckoning sign has the index finger sticking out of the clenched fist and palm facing the gesture. Then the speaker's finger moves repeatedly towards the gesturer as to invite something nearer. The beckoning sign has the general meaning of commanding someone to where you are standing. The beckoning sign is often performed with the four fingers using the entire hand, depending on how far the sign's recipient is. Depending on the circumstance, when performed with the index finger, it can have a sexual connotation.

If one feels that the speaker is not making sense, they are likely to keep their fingers straight and together while holding them upwards with the thumb pointing downwards. Then the fingers and thumb snap together to indicate a talking mouth. The gesture suggests contempt for a person talking for an excessive period about a topic that the gesturer feels is trivial. In Asian cultures, the gesture is used as a reaction to a dry joke. The gesture may also indicate that one is blabbering.

Also, there's the check signal that's caught on by servers around the world to flag that a supper supporter wishes to pay the charge and get out. The signal is showed by touching the record finger and thumb together and signifying a wavy line within the air associated with marking one's title. Drawing a checkmark within the discussion utilizing the fingers communicates that the person needs to pay the charge.

Chapter 5. Different Types of People and How They Fit In the Social Circle

All of us are full of different flaws that make us feel ashamed. We do have strengths that we want to brag about in front of everyone. Some of us prefer to stay natural in their everyday life while others love to take up their favorite persona to get through different hurdles in their lives. Some people like to make their way by deception, lies, and manipulation, while others prefer to face stumbling blocks but refuse to deviate from the right path. Whatever our choice of being a person in our lives is, the goal mustn't be of hiding our weaknesses and dark spots if we have any. We must allow our flaws to be a part of our personality. We should celebrate our flaws. It is what being human is about. When a person takes up a fake persona, he forgets that the people loving him are loving that persona that he has taken up and not that person who is in hiding under the fake personality. The real success is that people start loving us because of what we are and not because of what we are trying to become.

The Joker

The first category is a joker. The foremost feeling on hearing the word joker is of a person who is cracking jokes and laughing his heart out even during sober conversations. Jokers love jokes, costumes, and makeup. Each makeover gives them a new look and personality. They love to hide their real looks and nature from others. Generally, jokers are considered harmless, but things get different if we bring to mind batman's joker. A scary and nutty person comes to mind who is evil personified. That joker is always bent on inflicting the greatest pain on the people surrounding him. Can you think of a person who fulfills the above personality traits? Do you know anyone who laughs too much, always cracks jokes or tries to tease others while laughing it out? Beware! Jokers are masters of disguise.

The Smart One

Smart people can mold themselves according to the situation. They learn or are naturally gifted to adapt to changing circumstances. Smart people always remember to read other people's styles to gain more knowledge about them. They tend to see through the motives behind their acts and their hidden desires to work with them and gain benefits. Smart people are good at conveying their messages in an effective manner and without making the slightest buzz. They know how to express their feelings clearly, which is the most important thing when it comes to building and strengthening a relationship.

Similarly, smart people are very successful in their businesses or jobs. They work hard to learn how to read people, and the rest gets automatically easy for you. You can tell if a person is smart by looking at how they behave with you and other people around him. One important point to note is that smart people are very good at taking care of their interests, even at others' cost.

The Worker

Workers are the people who belong to a specific social class that is known for doing jobs for low pay only to live hand to mouth in their lives. The jobs they do low demand skills and labor and also have low literacy requirements. This category of people also lives off on social welfare programs. Working-class people mostly remain preoccupied with their day-to-day expenditures. They don't have time to take up different personas and disguises. Also, they are not smart enough to get a job done in the easiest way possible. Their brains are generally wired to do it the hard way. These people typically wear their hearts on their sleeves. They are easy to predict and are simple to understand.

The Loyal

These people are hard to find but exist. They are reliable as well as truthful. If a person is loyal to you, he shares affection with you and will not leave you when life gets hard for you. Loyal people think from their hearts and always work to benefit the people who are close to them. Just like the working class, loyal people are easily predictable and trustworthy.

The Strong

Physically strong people generally have a happy temperament. A strong person has higher levels of physical and mental strength. They don't have self-pity; that's why they are confident and good at judging people and dealing with them. Before they judge other people, they try to judge themselves. Besides, they have higher levels of self-restraint. Their nerves are powerful; that's why they are patient. They also are good listeners and observers. Their physical and mental strengths make them very good at reading other people and reaching an educated judgment. They don't hesitate to ask for help when they are in need, and also, they are open to helping others.

Different Types of Personalities

People are driven by their nature when they do this or leave you wondering why they did something that looked unwanted to you. It is perfectly normal if you think you need to understand someone a bit more than you already do. This someone can be a loved one or a person at our workplace. We have to accept the reality that people are not perfect. We are different, and it is this difference and diversity that makes this world a colorful and interesting place to live in. When people stay true to their role, they tend to contribute their bit to this diverse world. Imagine if we were all created in the same way, how the world looks like then. It would be boring.

Take an example of diversity. When a car hits a motorbike in a road accident, many people gather at the site. Most of them are on-lookers who are just investigating what happened. Some mourn the wounds of the injured while some call the ambulance. Only a handful of them step up and help the injured recover their senses. They try to administer to the first aid and take care of them until the ambulance arrives at the site. It is not that those people leap into a house on fire without thinking about their lives. We react differently to different situations. Our fears and desires trigger these reactions. Sometimes they motivate us, while at other times, they just demotivate us.

In analyzing people, you should know the people around you. What they do and how they react to different situations. Knowing their personality types and the fears that guide their behavior can improve how you interact with other people. It helps you read people more efficiently so that your interaction with them becomes smooth and your analysis of people broadens and deepens. Besides, you can track down your personality traits as well as faults. Let's roll on and take a look at different types of people in the world.

The Reformer/Idealist

The Reformer is a perfectionist. They have principles and are conscientious. These kinds of people have specific ideas to follow, and they come down hard on themselves and other people. They just love to keep them at pretty high standards. They are dedicated and responsible besides having perfect self-discipline.

They are usually successful in life because they tend to get lots of things to happen in a short time, and that too in the right way. They are always looking forward to setting themselves on the right path by eliminating their weaknesses. (9 Personality Types—Enneagram Numbers, nod)

The Performer

As the title suggests, these kinds of people will always be setting goals for themselves. They are highly target-oriented individuals, and they believe in doing rather than sitting on the couch and thinking day and night. They are always striving for success. This drive makes them pretty excellent at doing things right. You can find them in a big company, a shop or on the street selling vegetables or fruit. Wherever they are, their eyes are always on the horizon. They have dreams of success, and they are in the world to make them happen. These kinds of people are considered as role-models by many other people.

They have the fears that drive them toward the top. What makes them perfect is their urge to become somebody. The fear of dying as nobody makes them state-conscious. Instead of discouraging others, they respect the opinion of other people. (9 Personality Types—Enneagram Numbers, nod)

The Observer

These kinds of people spend time thinking and are of an introvert type. Their focus always is on gaining knowledge. They also prefer reading their personality instead of reading others. They remain absorbed in themselves and love to play with different types of concepts. They usually despise worldly attractions like big mansions, cars, and social status. They are always busy searching for themselves. They prefer to observe what is happening in their brains. You can see that these people will lock themselves in their rooms for hours as they love to understand how things go. This exclusive behavior allows them to concentrate on what they do. That's why they are usually considered experts on what they do. As they don't have the social skills needed to keep relationships healthy, they get overlooked most of the time.

The Adventurer

These kinds of people are fun-loving people. You will see them engaged in enjoyable pursuits, and also, they are often in an upbeat mood. They thrive on pleasure and adventures, which makes them a positive person. They tend to avoid negativity at all costs, which helps them fight off pessimism and stress well. They are also very optimistic and don't let tough challenges mar their optimism. They are the ones who always find that silver lining in dark clouds. They stick to that silver lining and turn negative situations fast and well. (9 Personality Types—Enneagram Numbers, nod)

Also, they are highly inconsistent. As they are fun-oriented, they remain in a particular work until the fun factor is alive but shoot out of it once they are bored, no matter if the work is complete or not. Completing projects poses a big challenge to them; that's why they struggle to succeed in the practical world.

The Warrior

As the name suggests, these kinds of people love to throw and take the gauntlet. They are strong and have dominating personalities. You can say they are born leaders and are confident. They are real alphas. They hate to depend on other people and also don't like to reveal their weaknesses. Instead, they use their strengths to cover those people who are around them as their family and friends. They are always ready to take charge of any situation, no matter how thundering and dreadful it is. They love to be the masters of their fate, and they also prefer to take control of people and circumstances.

Chapter 6: Body Language

If your mind is reeling from all the information shared so far, brace yourself. You see, this is an exceedingly vast topic. It is an essential topic because communication is one of the essential parts of our lives. How we communicate impacts our relationships, whether private, personal, or professional.

As with anything else, the impact can be positive or negative, so knowing what your body is saying on your behalf is of the utmost importance. The value in this book is not in learning all you need to know about this subject. It is in understanding that there is so much to know and that you can learn it over time by paying attention and putting in some effort.

Imagine that you are a very shy person who has amazing ideas for inventions or songs or movies, or whatever. Now, imagine how hard it would be for a very timid person to get those great ideas across to the right patent attorney, the right musician, or the right producer if they could barely speak above a whisper when they were nervous.

If they finally did get a meeting with their target audience, how would it look if they averted their eyes and crossed their arms over their body the whole time? Do you think they would be taken seriously? What is the possibility that they would win an influential person in a position of influence over under those circumstances?

There is nothing wrong with any personality type, but if you have a timid personality, know what your body language is saying on your behalf. If that is not what you want to convey, you can learn better behaviors that reflect what you want to say.

What of the person who is the opposite? What if you were naturally loud, bordering on boisterous, and the more nervous you became, the louder you seemed to get?

Being aware of how your volume affects others, you might try to tone it down a bit, but those who are naturally boisterous tend to have "big" body language as well.

If you walk into a room and begin to grip and shake hands as if you were arm wrestling, you would naturally start your event with mistrust and wariness as to your motives though you said very little at a modified decibel.

Here is one last word of caution about becoming a student of body language; never to use one cue to determine what a speaker means. Several factors are involved in each person's dynamic, and all must be considered before making an important determination.

Factors that could possibly affect someone's body language might include a physical or mental disability or limitation, a person's culture or background, or even a current health crisis.

Be aware that you can be influenced by body language with or without your consent, and you can influence others by your own body language, whether you are aware of it or even whether or not you mean to.

Body language is a powerful tool. Understand it and that understanding thoughtfully.

Chapter 7. Advanced Techniques to Manipulate Human Psychology

Sources tell us that it is concealment—hiding in the shadows, knowing when to strike. It is also a false front, hiding true intentions. When we are talking about this level of deception, we are talking about hiding aggression. When we take, there is a certain level of aggressive behavior that happens. A small part of manipulation is hiding that aggressive behavior so that the victim sees only good nature.

This is accomplished in various ways and means, one being knowledge. When we allow another to know us, we display vulnerability along with strengths. The experience of these personality traits can give the manipulator the ability to maneuver around without any alarms going off.

- The effectiveness of manipulating those strengths and vulnerabilities arrives when the dark practitioner knows what is vulnerable and inspires pride.

A reoccurring ideology that drives us to war takes into consideration that the action is more negative than positive. We want to avoid it. The manipulation process sees pride in all of us and plays to that pride. It is our strength. For example, when used to drive an army to slaughter others, the intention of our satisfaction has been manipulated to enforce the agendas of others.

- Often, the practitioners of dark psychology use aggression and fear to drive us. The less dark side still falls into the category of knowing what weakness is. That weakness leaves the individual open to control.

How the manipulator uses that control determines the severity of manipulation. There are positive versions of manipulating others, like convincing someone that they are not doing well and needing help. We, however, are looking at the darker side of this. The manipulator uses their control skills to get what they want—and the cost does not apply.

- There are many ways to move another into a place of being controlled. From the positive to the negative, psychological manipulators utilize all tactics.

When positive reinforcement is used, the charm is displayed. A forced smile or laughter can trigger laughter in all of us. As when we were infants, we copy what we see. When we see tears, we want them to stop. When we see a smile, we find ourselves smiling as well. Using positive reinforcement, the manipulator can shower money, charm, and gifts to get us to feel something. The usage of these things allows control of us on an instinctual level. We follow those who tell us what we want to hear.

- Psychological manipulation can also implement negative reinforcement. This is a form of deflection—the substitution of one thing for another.

Often, we have things we need or have to do, and we do not want to do them. The psychological manipulation of negative reinforcement uses that power of negativity to lure the subject from their original need, pushing them toward something they want to be done instead. The long game, a slow play of putting tasks into another's life and then controlling those tasks so that the manipulator can get what they want, is an extraordinarily useful and subdued tactic. Sometimes only partial reinforcement is required to gain control. We are talking about elevating the fear or doubt regarding the tasks needed to be done. The partial is the extended play. It knows that in the end, the victim will lose. It knows that by planting small seeds now, victory will eventually happen. It knows that we all have our weaknesses and that by planting even a tiny seed, we can take someone to that weakness. An individual trying to work toward something they already were shaky on or had doubts about will listen to the lie and flow with that idea, and use it to their destruction.

- The partial manipulator only needs to put the thought in mind, knowing the weakness is already there, and utilizing it will take their prey to a destructive end.

Psychological manipulators flat, outright punish. From an actual physical lashing to the victim's passive-aggressive playing, punishment is beneficial when one wants to control another.

- We skulk and cry and yell and nag and go completely silent. This is the blackmail of the manipulator. It inspires guilt in us. That "wanting to be the better person" rises to the front, and we do what the manipulator wants. When the manipulator sets free the crocodile tears, we have no idea if they are real or not. The degree of crying is not up to us to determine. Only the manipulator knows if the tears are legitimate or not. In this case, the trap is often sprung from the victim's side. They walk up to the hurt individual to help, only to find that the manipulator is just lying in wait to strike.

- One extreme version of manipulation is violence.

Violence triggers something inside us. We often do anything to avoid it. The manipulator knows that power strategically applied can make us go into a state of avoidance. There incites the control, physical violence can have mental scarring, and the manipulator causes the scarring. It places power in tactical places to get the result they want.

Some would say this is the darkest of the dark. Taken to the individual, this can mentally damage them for an extended period, if not permanently. Placed on a world stage, it can lead up to the physical conflict of genocide.

- Mostly, it is about gain. Manipulators of the dark want to gain something. When we speak about improvement, we are talking about power and influence, control and manipulation over others. The trophy is up to the individual. This can be everything as to gaining affections, to money, and even to life itself.

It is about gaining for their reasons and gratifications. The taking of others and making the power and control their own. Selfishness to the extreme. The mind of the dark practitioner sees the ultimate win as the gain over others. They have power. Superiority is the power over another, and taking of someone else's power makes them feel superior. This is a tremendous driving force behind the manipulator. Often, in the case of immature individuals driving manipulations toward superiority, any is pushed aside for just the feeling of being superior. In relationships, it is about control. The manipulation of power can put one in control. Although we have looked at the vampire and energy role, we know who has control.

This feeling of control can be overwhelming to the mental state of the dark. Almost drug-like, it is a feeling of emotion that is more logical. Management is one of the most straightforward manipulation tactics to achieve with only logic to guide. It drives not only the victim but the manipulator as well. Psychological manipulation can also be about self-esteem. The self of the manipulator is always in question. This is one of the reasons they manipulate, to define themselves. How easily they can manage, another can tell the dark that they are better than others. That weakness and strength can be measured in the tactical playing field of the hustle.

- The dark psychological manipulator is bored most of the time, more than most. The psychological manipulator will often use manipulation to determine the validity of feelings and emotions.

This boils down to that manipulation applied in relations with others helps the manipulator regulate reactions to validate or not validate their own emotions. The manipulator measures the self and their self-esteem by how others handle their self-questioning. This happens when the practitioner does not have a grasp on what emotions are. They look at their feelings as invalid and manipulate the situation in such a way as to validate them. We are stuck with ourselves, and we cannot get away. Psychological manipulators validate or invalidate themselves by the tactical controlling of others. It is an exciting way of viewing life, although we all idolize one form of manipulation.

- **The con aspect.** One common form of manipulation is the convincing of another to make their money's yours. This is a hidden agenda of the criminal. This form of mental manipulation preys mostly on the elderly and the rich. However, we all can fall into this form of manipulation. We choose to spend on, and we do not respond to a state of psychological manipulation.

Something happens when the buck is passed over, we go from manipulation into action, and something drives us. It is within us, and it is outside forces that drive. What causes this drive and the drive itself is called Persuasion.

The manipulation process in dark psychology usually is not a single move. It is a complex series of actions, often with the outcome only known by the manipulator. The motivations of manipulators are as convoluted as human nature.

Chapter 8. Mind Control

Mind control is an aspect of manipulation that is similar to brainwashing. The main difference is that the individual might only want to control your mind at the moment. Maybe they want to get you to do something that will benefit them temporarily because they are opportunistic individuals. Since there is not much time to take over a person's mind when you are engaged in a simple conversation, there are some very detailed techniques that a manipulator will use to attempt to gain control of your mind. As you explore these techniques, you will also learn how to combat each of them. The stronger your reason is, the better you will ward off the people trying to harm you.

Compensating for Lack of Physical Prowess

Someone might try to control your mind because you secretly intimate them. Because someone does not appear physically threatening, a manipulator will be quick to move forward with mind control by seeing how much they can change your thoughts. The mind control gives them the same type of satisfaction they would receive if they were physically controlling you. Because the latter is a lot more prominent, the idea of controlling your mind is also a lot more appealing. You will find that manipulators are very discreet about this.

They might remark on how strong or tough you are, building you up based on your physical characteristics. Even a simple comment about you being tall can be enough to let you think that they respect you because you have more physical prowess than they do—this is what they want you to think. Instead of backing down, which you will think they are doing, they make you more vulnerable by making you comfortable.

When you believe that someone sees powerful traits in you, you will be less likely to assume that they have bad intentions. Surely because they appear to respect you, they won't deceive you, right? Always make sure that you remind yourself anyone can fool you at any time. It is hard to keep track of everyone's true intentions, especially when they have mastered the art of mind control.

What You Can Do: Remain firm in your core beliefs. Even if you believe that the individual respects you and what you stand for, always remind yourself of what you hold dear to your heart. Staying true to who you give you little reason to change your opinions on a whim. Remind yourself that the person trying to control your mind is very insecure.

Using Hand Placement as a Decoy

Have you ever noticed that people normally place their fingers on their heads when thinking very hard? In moments of concentration, you have probably done the same thing. This is a subconscious mind control technique that is often used by manipulators. When they want you to rethink something, they might place their fingers on their head to coax you into doing the same. With the help of muscle memory, your brain will be receiving a message that it needs to think harder.

It is an interesting technique because it is so subtle. You surely would not notice it if you were not looking for it in the first place. As you become better at reading body language, you will become more aware of moments when the person you are talking to is merely using a decoy movement as an attempt to control you. Do your best to break the mirroring effect that typically happens during a conversation. Keep your arms in a neutral position by your side.

Manipulators get nervous. They probably get very nervous and will do the best they can to hide this from you. As soon as you notice their fingers move up to their head, imagine that they are nervous that they won't be able to pull off this attempt at mind control. Pride yourself in your ability to pick up on it before it affects you—this will keep you strong.

What You Can Do: In an attempt to break their cycle, you can make a comment that indirectly refers to them concentrating. Something like, "Oh, is that what you were thinking?" is a way to make manipulators second-guess their abilities. If you let them know from the start that you are not automatically going to agree with what they are saying, this will be your way of standing your ground.

Convincing You of Psychic Powers

The person who is manipulating you is not any more powerful than you—repeat this to yourself often. Even though many mind controllers are portrayed as psychic beings, this is not the case for most. A successful manipulator is usually just very good at picking up on your body language and context. There is nothing psychic about it, though it can feel that way at times.

Being misinformed that someone is psychic and can read your mind at any time is intimidating. These are your private thoughts, and you do not want anyone intruding upon them. The good news is that you never have to let this happen. You are still in control of your inner thoughts, and what you share with the world is always going to be your decision. Anyone who tries to force you or to coax you into sharing something you do not want to does not have your best interest at heart.

The mention of psychic abilities might come up as a joke. For example, the manipulator will joke around with you while mentioning that you don't need to say much because they already know what you are thinking. You can laugh this off, but you can also remain firm in believing that this isn't true. With the way you portray yourself, you can get them to think anything you want.

What You Can Do: Always be aware of your intention during every conversation. If you are presenting yourself in a certain way, the manipulative person will pick up on it. Try your hardest to practice standing neutrally and speaking neutrally. When you can master this concept, it will be a lot harder for them to read you.

Surrounding You with Other Manipulative People

This is an incredibly dangerous mind-control technique because it closely ties in with the idea behind brainwashing. The more people that you believe are on the same page about something will make you want to agree with them, too. If a manipulator can find other people who want to manipulate a vulnerable person, you might become an easy target for a bad situation. They will gang up on you in a way that is subtle yet effective. You do not have to put up with this. Knowing who you are as a person will protect you in many ways.

There will be times when a manipulator will only "scout" for like-minded individuals that believe in the point they are making. Unknowingly, they might recruit innocent bystanders to further lead you into thinking that you must agree with them. The people that also fall victim to these traps might be people you love and respect. This is why it might be tempting to give in and to just "go with the flow." It is what the manipulator wants you to think. They want others to know that it is easier to go with a mass opinion than form their own.

What You Can Do: Speak up when you disagree with something. This is difficult because you do not want to cause conflict or controversy, but it becomes necessary to protect yourself. A disagreement does not always have to turn into an argument. If you approach the situation maturely, you can simply speak your mind to get your point across without requiring validation. You can provide this for yourself. Remind yourself that it is not other people's opinions that matter most. Your view of yourself dictates your self-esteem.

Believing it Won't Happen to You

Because a mind controller works hard to use other people, you might assume that they would instead do this to strangers or bystanders. One of the most challenging realities to face is that these individuals are more likely to attempt the act of mind control on a loved one. This happens because the task seems a lot easier—they already know you well. Instead of having to figure out the things that get under your skin, they have an idea of what to say and how to persuade you. Realizing this can be very hurtful, especially when you have many trusts invested in the person.

"I would never do anything to hurt you" is a promise that is often broken by a manipulator. With mind control, they are directly going against that promise, even if it doesn't feel hurtful at the moment. When someone does not respect you for who you are, they will do anything to change you. Suggesting you should get something else to eat or that you should shop elsewhere for clothing are two simple examples of how manipulators can use their conviction to change you.

You might not believe that these little changes mean much, but when you add them up, they can completely transform who you are as a person. It is not a great feeling to realize that you no longer recognize who you are. As upsetting as it is, you have to work on rebuilding yourself and getting back to your roots. It is normal to feel betrayed because this is what the manipulator has done to you—betrayed your trust.

What You Can Do: Never let your naive thinking get in the way of your rational thinking. You are not immune to the mind control that goes on around you. Your strength does not necessarily protect you from the intentions of all manipulators. By keeping yourself humble, you will always be on alert for the red flags presented by those who wish to change your mind.

The Blank Stares of Intimidation

Making a statement to someone and receiving a blank stare in return is intimidating for many reasons. One of the most prominent is that you do not know what they are thinking. It scares you because you might not know what to say or do next. A manipulator will use this technique to control your mind after you have said something vulnerable or profound. This will make you second-guess if what you said was "wrong" or incorrect somehow. You will end up prioritizing their feelings over your own.

They might follow this instance up with a statement that seems wise or all-knowing. When you combine the two actions, you are sure to believe that they can read your mind or that they know something you don't know. Both possibilities are unsettling in their ways. When you feel a negative emotion, understand that this is what your manipulator wants you to feel. They want to catch you off-guard and make you question everything that you have confirmed in your reality. By slowly breaking you down and staring at you blankly, you will get the idea that you came to this conclusion independently. It becomes maddening when you do not realize what is happening to you.

Chapter 9. Mind Control Techniques

Mind control involves using influence and persuasion to change the behaviors and beliefs of someone. That someone might be the person themselves, or it might be someone else. Mind control has also been referred to as brainwashing, thought reform, coercive persuasion, mental control, and manipulation, just to name a few. Some people feel that everything is done by manipulation. But if that is true to be believed, then important points about manipulation will be lost. Influence is much better thought of as a mental continuum with two extremes. One side has respectful and ethical influences and works to improve the individual while showing respect for them and their basic human rights. The other side contains dark and destructive influences that work to remove that human rights from a person, such as independence, rational thought, and sometimes their real identity.

When thinking of mind control, it is better to see it use influence on other people to disrupt something in them, as their way of thinking or living. The influence works based on what makes people human, such as their behaviors, beliefs, and values. It can disrupt the very way they chose personal preferences or make critical decisions. Mind control is nothing more than using words and ideas to convince someone to say or do something they might never have thought of saying or doing on their own.

There are scientifically proven methods that can be used to influence other people. Mind control has nothing to do with fakery, ancient arts, or even magical powers. Real mind control is the basis of a word that many people hate to hear. That word is marketing. Many people hate to hear that word because of the negative connotations associated with it. When people hear "marketing," they automatically assume that it refers to those ideas taught in business school. But the basis of marketing is not about deciding which part of the market to target or deciding which customers will likely buy this product. The basis of marketing is one very simple word. That word is "YES."

If a salesperson asks a regular customer to write a brief endorsement of the product they buy, they will hopefully say yes. If someone asks their significant other to take some of the business cards to pass out at work, they will hopefully say yes. If you write any blog and ask another blogger to provide a link to yours on their blog, they will hopefully say yes. When enough people say yes, the business or blog will begin to grow. With even more yesses, it will continue to grow and thrive. This is the very simple basis of marketing. Marketing is nothing more than using mind control to get other people to buy something or do something beneficial. And the techniques can easily be learned.

The first technique in mind control is to tell people what you want them to want. Never tell people to think it over or take some time. That is a definite mind control killer. People already have too much going on in their minds. When they are told to think something over, they will not. It will be forgotten, and then it will never happen. This has nothing to do with being stupid or lazy and everything to do with just being way too busy.

So the best strategy is to take the offensive and think for them. Everything must be explained in the beginning. Never assume that the other blogger will automatically understand the benefits of adding a link will be for them. Do not expect anyone to give a demonstration blindly. And merely asking for a testimonial, while it might garner an appositive response, probably will not garner a well-formed testimonial to the product. Instead, be prepared to explain the blog, show examples, and offer compelling reasons why this merger will benefit both parties. Have the demonstration laid out in great detail with notes on what to say when and visuals to go along with the letters, so all the other person has to do is present the information. Offer the customer a few testimonials that have already been received and ask them to choose one and personalize it a bit. Always be specific in explaining what is desired. Explain why it is desired. Show how this will work. Tell the person how to do it and why they should do it. If done correctly, it will feel exactly like one friend advising another friend on which is the best path to take. And the answer will be yes, simply because saying yes makes so much sense.

Think of the avalanche. Think of climbing all the way to the top of the highest mountain ever. Now, at the top, think of searching for the biggest, heaviest boulder on the mountain. Now, picture summoning up superhuman strength to push this boulder, dislodging it from the place it has rested for years and years. Once this boulder is loosened, it rolls easily over the edge of the cliff, crashing into thousands of other boulders on its way down the mountain, taking half of the mountain with it in a beautiful cascade of rocks and dirt. Imagine sitting there, smiling cheerfully at the avalanche that was just created.

Marketing and mind control are very like creating an avalanche. Getting the first person to answer yes might be difficult. But each subsequent yes will be easier. Always start at the top, never the bottom. Starting at the top is more complicated. It is more likely to come with more negative responses than positive responses in the beginning. But starting at the top also yields a much greater reward when the avalanche does begin. And the results will be far greater than beginning at the bottom of the mountain. Yes, the small rock is easier to push over. Then it can be built upon by pushing over another small rock, then another. This way can work, but it will take much longer than being successful at the top. No one ever went fishing for the smallest fish in the pond or auditioned for the secondary role just to be safe. Everyone wants that top prize. Do not be afraid to go for it.

On the other hand, never ask for the whole boulder the first time. Ask for part of it. This may seem directly contradictory, but it is not. Always start with a small piece. Make the beginning easier for everyone to see. Let other people use their insight to see the result. When the first bit goes well, then gradually ask for more and more and more.

Think of writing a guest spot for someone else who has their own blog. By sending in the entire manuscript first, there is a greater risk of rejection. Begin small. Send them a paragraph or two discussing them with the idea. Then outline the idea and send that in an email. Then write the complete draft you would like them to use and send it along. When asking a customer for a testimonial, start by asking for a few lines in an email. Then ask the customer to expand those few lines into a testimonial covering at least half a typed page. The customer will soon be ready for an hour-long webcast extolling the product's virtues and your great customer service skills.

Everything must have a deadline that exists. The important word here is the word 'real.' Everyone has heard the salesperson who said to decide right away because the deal might not be available later or another customer was coming in, and they might get it. That is a total fabrication, and everyone knows it to be true. There are no impending other customers, and the deal is not going to disappear. There is no real sense of urgency involved. But everyone does it. There are too many situations where people are given a fake deadline by someone who thinks it will instill a great sense of urgency for completing the task. It is not only totally not effective but completely unneeded. It is a simple matter to create true urgency. Only leave free things available for a finite amount of time. When asking customers for testimonials, be certain to mention the last possible day for it to be received to be able to be used. Some people will be unable to assist, but having people unable to participate is better than never beginning.

Always give before you receive it. And do not ever think that giving is fifty-fifty. Always give much more than is expected in return. Before asking for a testimonial from a satisfied customer, be sure to make numerous acts of exceptional customer service. Before asking a blog writer for a link, link theirs to yours many times. This is not about helping someone out so that they will help you. This is all about being so totally generous that the person who is asked for the favor cannot possibly say no. It might mean extra work, but that is how to influence other people.

Always stand up for something much bigger than average. Do not just write another blog on how to do something. Use a critical issue to take a stand and defend the stance with unbeatable logic and genuine passion. Do not just write a how-to manual. Choose a particular idea and sell people on it, using examples of other people with the same idea living the philosophy.

Never feel shame. This does not mean being extremely extroverted to the point of silliness or having a total lack of conscience in business dealings. In mind control, shamelessness refers to a full, complete belief that this course of action is the best possible course. Everyone will benefit greatly from it. This is about writing the best possible blog ever and believing that everyone needs to read it to improve their lives. It is about believing in a particular product so deeply that the feeling is that everyone will benefit from using it. Knowing deep inside that this belief is the correct belief ever and everyone should believe it.

Mind control uses the idea that someone's decisions and emotions can be controlled using psychological means. It uses negotiation or mental influence powers to ensure the outcome of the interaction is more favorable to one person over the other. This is what marketing is: convincing someone to do something particular or buy something in particular. Being able to control someone else's mind merely means understanding the power of human emotion and playing upon those emotions. It is easier to have a mental impact on people if there is a basic understanding of human emotions. Angry people will back down when the subject of their anger is not afraid. Angry people feed upon the fear of others.

Chapter 10. Influence People With Mind Control

A mind controller approaches the victim with the sole intent of cloning themselves, making the other person think like them. This is a complicated thing to do, so, to achieve it, one has to possess an inflated ego, lack doubts about themselves, and have a high sense of entitlement. All of us are susceptible to manipulation, and what matters is how much effect the mind control will have on us.

Psychologists studying mind control have found out that the entire process seems to adhere to a typical structure. This conclusion was made after a study was conducted on multiple marketing and networking companies which used mind control to persuade clients to purchase their products. One of the remarkable similarities is that all new members joining the companies underwent pre-planned training to recruit more people and convince potential customers to buy their products. The training sessions are meant to make the employees think like the company wants and use a mind twist to convince people.

Let us now look at the mind control process in detail:

Step 1: Understanding the target

Before anything else, the manipulator will seek to establish a bond or connection with their potential victim. Good intent, or friendship, will be the first step because it makes the victim lower all their social and psychological defenses. Once the controller gains the target's trust, they start reading them to devise the most effective method to invade them. The reading aims to tell whether their victim is susceptible to their manipulation. Just like any project manager, they do not like wasting time on a subject they suspect might outsmart them and lead to failure.

Multiple clues are used to scan the victim. They include vocal style, body language, social status, gender, emotional stability, etc. A person's traits can be used to decode the strength of their defenses. All this time, the manipulator will be asking themselves questions like, "Are you introvert or extrovert?" "Are you weakly?" "Are you emotional?" "Are you self-confident?" Humans give a lot of information about themselves when interacting with each other. This is something that the controller knows all too well. From these signs, they can quickly tell if the person is cooperating. They will look at body posture and immediately analyze the victim. Excess blinking might insinuate that a person is lying. Arms folded across the chest might show a lack of interest or insecurity. Taking enormous strides while walking might portray fear. As you can see, the body releases so much data at any given time that it is essential to be aware of the signs that you are giving out

When the attacker has collected enough data from the target, they now understand their interests, strengths, weaknesses, routines, and so on. Using this information, they can decide on an entry point, which will allow for easy and accurate manipulation. They also determine whether the target is worth the effort. If they see one as a favorable target, they move to the other step in the mind control process- unfreezing factual beliefs and values.

Step 2: Unfreezing Solid Beliefs and Values

All of us have some beliefs and values engraved deep within. Most of them are the principles that were instilled in us since childhood, and others have been acquired from experiences are we grow older. We rarely let go of them, but revise them as we proceed. Most of them make up our identities, so we do not like them being interfered with. If these principles are threatened, contradicted, or questioned at any point in time, our natural reaction is to defend them through all means possible. However, if a good-enough reason is given to us, so we voluntarily question them ourselves; we undergo a process known as "unfreezing."

Tons of reasons can lead us to unfreeze: a breakup, the death of a loved one, religious interference, getting evicted from our houses, to mention but a few. These situations force us to seek answers to complex cases, which goes as deep as questioning our sole beliefs and values. Take this, for example:

Way back when I am a teenager, we had some family friends who were solid Christians. It happens that my best friend, who was my exact age, came from this family. His name was Sam. Sam used to tell me about the Bible and its teachings, trying to convince me to accept salvation and live according to its instructions. I remember asking him why he was so insistent on this issue. He would respond that all problems were solvable with saving and that life was much more comfortable and happier. Fast-forward about fifteen years, Sam's mother was diagnosed with breast cancer. They tried all forms of treatment available at the time, but the cancer would grow back. One day, while talking to him about the issue, he looked at me with a pale face and said, "I think what they say about Christianity is not real!" Unsure about what he had just said, I asked him why he thought so. He responded that they had met tens of spiritual leaders for prayers, but his mother's cancer was only getting worse. What's worse, she would not live for more than a year.

Sad as Sam's story is, it makes us realize that some situations in life might force us to question the vital principles that we grow up with. In this case, my best friend had come to doubt the very same religion that he once felt had automatic solutions to all of life's problems. In the very same manner, a manipulator will dig deep into their victim's life to understand their vulnerabilities and exploit them fully. These people will say anything they think their targets would love to hear. Once the victim swallows the manipulator's comfort, there is a shift in power dynamics, and the target is now ready for the manipulation.

Step 3: Reprogramming the Mind

The mind control process seeks to separate the target from their initial beliefs and begin reprogramming their mind. The reprogramming is meant to install the manipulator's beliefs and values into the victim's mind. Apart from distancing the initial principles, the controller also tries their best to make them look wrong or harmful, or the cause of past mishaps in the victim's life. If the victim absorbs this reprogramming, their defense is lowered to zero, and they now become a robot that is ready to accept any operating system that is offered.

During the reprogramming phase, the attacker will ensure the victim has minimal contact with the outside world. They make everyone else appear insignificant to the victim because this raises their opportunity to deposit their malicious principles. This behavior is typical in cults, mostly crafted to sway their followers from mainstream human life. Some cults go as far as controlling their followers' food intake as a way of weakening them. The psychology behind this idea is that a weak person will always turn to the person they feel has the power to protect them or alleviate their suffering. The same happens in relationships, where one partner plays the controlling role. The victimized one has no choice but to adhere to the other. You might wonder why some people put up with violent partners. Still, so far, you must already understand that the problem is more profound than it appears. If you control a person's mind, you can control their lives.

Once the victim has been reprogrammed, the manipulator moves into the final phase of the mind control process known as "freezing."

Step 4: Freezing the New Beliefs and Values

Once the victim has been fed with contrasting principles by the offender, the offender applies tactics to cement the new beliefs into their brains. This is what psychologists call "freezing." The freezing bit is necessary because the controller is aware of the person's original ideas that might clash with their initial ones. As such, they need to force the victim to choose their malicious principles over their old ones. To do this, they might apply any of the following methods.

One of the methods is using the reward/punishment approach. When the victim acts according to the manipulator's demands, they are rewarded. Hopefully, you see the similarity between the freezing process and dog training. The dog is given treats when it follows the trainer's instructions. The trainer aims at solidifying the new skill in the dog by rewarding it. In the future, if the dog is instructed to do the same thing, it will not hesitate since it has been made to think that obeying the command is useful and attracts a reward. The same applies to mind control; when the victim follows, they are made to feel that what they did was right and deserves a reward.

Punishments are the second most-applied approach in the freezing process. If the victim deviates from the controller's commands, they are punished. If we go back to a cult scenario, they usually have defined punishments for violations of terms. During the Holocaust, for instance, any Germans who failed to hail Hitler were punished through imprisonment or death. In the same way, any German who was suspected of protecting the Jews was shot. Hitler understood that by punishing anyone who went against his rules, he would force every German to help him attain his ethnic cleansing objective. The psychological trick used in these situations is that the victim is made to see punishment as justice being served for breaking the rules.

Mind controllers' final method to solidify their manipulation is to transform their victims into their agents. Better put, once the controller feels that the victim's pseudo personality has materialized, they use them to distribute their worldviews. We said that the mind controller's list is to create a replica of themselves in the other person. Therefore, once the controlling process is complete, the victim starts living like the attacker without realizing it. Depending on the manipulation's nature, the victim might also be used to recruit more victims into the oppressor's way of thinking and living. This is especially true in the context of marketing and networking. From this explanation, we can readily tell why a wife is likely to be violent towards the kids if the husband is violent. The kids are also expected to be violent towards each other or their friends. The process of mind control is slow, but once it solidifies, it can result in devastating effects.

Conclusion

Whenever folks try to provide meaning to the notion of demeanor, their responses always come in various forms. Even though some could put their thoughts on the ads and advertisements which are everywhere in contemporary society, advocating you to patronize a specific product or service over the other others' heads fall back into the politicians who attempt to modify the minds of Republicans simply to get yet another vote in the polls. Both instances are right since they are messages targeted at altering the understanding of this topic. The purpose of diversion between ordinary persuasion and dim persuasion is the dark persuasion doesn't necessarily have a moral rationale.

Even though a standard persuader might attempt to convince someone for this individual's own great, a dim persuader does so together with motives that are not always great for another individual. They try to obtain a total grasp of the individual they would like to convince and take pains to do this since they understand the greatest motivation.

While persuasion consistently has ethical consequences, a dim persuader doesn't concern themselves with those consequences. In reality, they are mindful of these, but decide to put their eyes on their goal (s) rather than persuasion as a mental phenomenon in an individual's regular life. It's either that you're the person attempting to convince someone else or you're being persuaded. What makes the distinction between dark and ordinary is that the motivation for this. In mass media, politics, legal and advertising conclusions, persuasion comes to play all of the time. The results of instructing it in such areas are set utilizing persuasion to determine the topic of influence.

There are a few clear and crucial differences between behavioral and other brain control varieties, like brainwashing and hypnosis. Even though these two demands that the topic should be isolated from modifying their thoughts and individuality, persuasion doesn't require isolation. To be able to reach the target, manipulation is utilized on a single individual. Although persuasion may also be performed on a single topic to make them change their thoughts, there's also a chance of using it on a vast scale to alter the heads of an entire group or a whole society.

Because of this, persuasion is a much better mind control procedure and maybe more harmful since it can alter the minds of lots of people at precisely the same time rather than the head of only one individual at one time. Many people produce the error of believing that they have immunity to the consequences of persuasion because they think that they will always have the ability to observe every sales pitch that comes in their way.

They think they'll always have the ability to use logic to grasp what's happening and find a logical decision for this. As a result of how people aren't ever likely to fall for whatever they hear, this might be accurate if they utilize logic. It's likewise feasible to steer clear of persuasion since the debate doesn't augur nicely with the individual's beliefs, whatever the strength of this debate. Some individuals understand how to use clear messages to inspire people to market the industry's newest gadgets or goods. This information action is quite delicate, so the topic won't always recognize it; therefore, it's going to be rather difficult for them to continually have the ability to decide the information they will get.

Every time is said, it's extremely probable that you think about it in a terrible light. That is because it is inclined to automatically consider a conman or salesman who's always attempting to make them modify their view, and that will finally push them till this shift is reached. While black persuasion is notable in earnings and conning clinics, also, there are ways that persuasion may be used permanently, such as in diplomatic relationships between global bodies or at public service attempts. The difference only lies in the method by which in which the practice of persuasion is attracted to perform.

Dark Persuasion Methods

When an individual is prepared to modify the head of the topic by devoting them to do anything against their first frame of mind, the persuader will get some nicely laid out methods to help them reach their targets. Every day that passes, the goal will face various kinds of persuasion. Food manufacturers aim to receive their goal to test the recipes that are new or have them adhere to the earlier ones, even while studios may flaunt their most recent blockbuster films about the faces of the aims. In any situation may be whatever merchandise they're promoting, their principal intent is to generate more revenue, and that's the reason they're attempting to convince you. They couldn't care less about how this may affect you, and that is why they need to be quite careful and proficient in the art of subtle persuasion to make sure they don't deceive you off or make you plump.

As there are also lots of different brands attempting to convince you, they need to locate an exceptional approach to impress their perspectives on you. As a result of the effect of info on a vast selection of individuals, the methods used in it's been a topic of research for several decades, dating back to early times. That is because the influence is a really helpful instrument in controlling a large assortment of individuals. Beginning in the early 20th century, the proper analysis of those techniques started to grow. Bear in mind that the objective of attempting to convince people would be to push a compelling debate in an audience and have the positive.

They'll then internalize this information and embrace it as their fresh mindset or even means of life. Because of this, there's a great need to find very prosperous persuasion methods. Three dark persuasion methods are of fantastic value through recent years. We will go over those three:

Create a Need

This is only one of the most profitable methods of obtaining an individual to change their perspective or lifestyle. The individual hoping to convince a goal will create demand or concentrate on a demand that the topic already has. If that is achieved suitably, it's the capacity of enticing a fantastic deal to your goal. This signifies that to become prosperous, the persuader should interest in the demands that are far more significant to the goal.

This could be their requirement to fulfill their fantasies of fostering their self-esteem. It might also function as a desire for love, food, or shelter. This method will work out nicely since there's not anyway the topic isn't likely to require one or more of these items or need of anything at all for that matter. As there's not always, the goal is not likely to get dreams and ambitions. The persuader will probably simply find strategies to produce the sufferer understand how they can easily help the sufferer attain those dreams. The persuader can also tell their goal the goal will probably recognize their visions if they make certain adjustments to their faith or outlook.

As stated by the persuader, doing this will provide the target with a greater prospect of attaining success. For example, a young guy who wishes to get romantic with a woman may inform her that he'll help her boost her grades and eventually make her parents happy by obtaining a. Still, only when she's friends with his or her although this woman may believe she has finally discovered the salvation she desires, the simple truth is that the young guy is not very curious about how she plays in college. Her teenagers are just a lure for obtaining access to sexual activity.

Appealing to Social Needs

Another technique the persuader may utilize is identifying the goal of social demands. Even though this might not yield as many outcomes and the goal's main requirements will, it's still a powerful instrument in the hands of the persuader. Some are naturally attracted to audiences and want to be desired. They always wish for certain things, not because they want them, but because it includes certain prestige, making them feel like they belong to a bigger course. The idea of appealing to your target's societal needs is what's accessible through several TV advertisements where audiences are invited to purchase a product so they won't be "left behind." When they could recognize and allure to the societal needs of their goal, the outcome is that they can achieve a new field of the goal's interest.

Making Use of Loaded Words and Images

When an individual is hoping to convince someone else, they need to be cautious with their selection of words because words could make all of the difference. When there are many means to say something, one way of stating it might be more potent than another. When it's related to persuasion, among the essential things is understanding how to say the ideal thing at the ideal moment. Words are the most effective tools in communicating and understanding the perfect call-to-action phrases.

Dark persuasion is just one of the most effective dim psychology theories, but regrettably, it's always overlooked and suppressed. This might be because, unlike many different head control procedures, persuasion renders the goal using a selection. At another mind control procedure, the aim is forced to enter.

Occasionally, this is achieved by placing them into isolation to ensure, in conclusion, they don't have any say in the procedure results. Regarding persuasion, the chips have been laid bare (though with the ulterior purpose in dim persuasion), so the goal is made to make the choice they think will fit them best.

www.ingramcontent.com/pod-product-compliance
Lightning Source LLC
Chambersburg PA
CBHW071123030426
42336CB00013BA/2190